ALL ABOUT INSECTS
ALL ABOUT CICADAS

by Golriz Golkar

Ideas for Parents and Teachers

Pogo Books let children practice reading informational text while introducing them to nonfiction features such as headings, labels, sidebars, maps, and diagrams, as well as a table of contents, glossary, and index.

Carefully leveled text with a strong photo match offers early fluent readers the support they need to succeed.

Before Reading

- "Walk" through the book and point out the various nonfiction features. Ask the student what purpose each feature serves.
- Look at the glossary together. Read and discuss the words.

Read the Book

- Have the child read the book independently.
- Invite him or her to list questions that arise from reading.

After Reading

- Discuss the child's questions. Talk about how he or she might find answers to those questions.
- Prompt the child to think more. Ask: Have you ever heard cicadas? What did they sound like?

Pogo Books are published by Jump!
5357 Penn Avenue South
Minneapolis, MN 55419
www.jumplibrary.com

Copyright © 2025 Jump!
International copyright reserved in all countries. No part of this book may be reproduced in any form without written permission from the publisher.

Library of Congress Cataloging-in-Publication Data

Names: Golkar, Golriz, author.
Title: All about cicadas / by Golriz Golkar.
Description: Minneapolis, MN: Jump!, Inc., [2025]
Series: All about insects | Includes index.
Audience: Ages 7-10
Identifiers: LCCN 2023050540 (print)
LCCN 2023050541 (ebook)
ISBN 9798889969785 (hardcover)
ISBN 9798889969792 (paperback)
ISBN 9798889969808 (ebook)
Subjects: LCSH: Cicadas—Juvenile literature.
Cicadas—Life cycles—Juvenile literature.
Classification: LCC QL527.C5 G65 2025 (print)
LCC QL527.C5 (ebook)
DDC 595.7/52—dc23/eng/20231204
LC record available at https://lccn.loc.gov/2023050540
LC ebook record available at https://lccn.loc.gov/2023050541

Editor: Katie Chanez
Designer: Emma Almgren-Bersie

Photo Credits: eye-blink/iStock, cover; suradech123yim/Shutterstock, 1; xpixel/Shutterstock, 3; 24Novembers/Shutterstock, 4; rbmiles/iStock, 5; Mark Brandon/Shutterstock, 6-7; Aaskolnick/Dreamstime, 8 (cicada); Christina Rowe/Wikimedia, 8 (eggs); Gerry Bishop/Shutterstock, 9; Souchon Yves/Shutterstock, 10-11; David Des Rochers/Dreamstime, 12-13; sankai/iStock, 14-15; Auscape/Universal Images Group/Getty, 16; D Frank Wright/iStock, 17; Doug Wechsler/Nature Picture Library, 18-19; HKPNC/iStock, 20-21; Luc Pouliot/Shutterstock, 23.

Printed in the United States of America at Corporate Graphics in North Mankato, Minnesota.

TABLE OF CONTENTS

CHAPTER 1
Hey, Cicada!...4

CHAPTER 2
Life Cycle..8

CHAPTER 3
Life Above the Ground................................16

ACTIVITIES & TOOLS
Try This!...22
Glossary...23
Index..24
To Learn More...24

CHAPTER 1
HEY, CICADA!

A big **insect** lands on a rock. Four wings fold across its back. What is this insect? It is a cicada!

There are more than 3,000 cicada **species**. They spend most of their lives underground. They come up in summer. Many come up at the same time. They cover plants. Sometimes they cover cars and homes!

CHAPTER 1

Cicadas are noisy. Males have tymbals. These are on the abdomen. They shake. This makes a loud buzzing sound. Females do not have them. To make noise, they click their wings.

TAKE A LOOK!

What are the parts of a male cicada? Take a look!

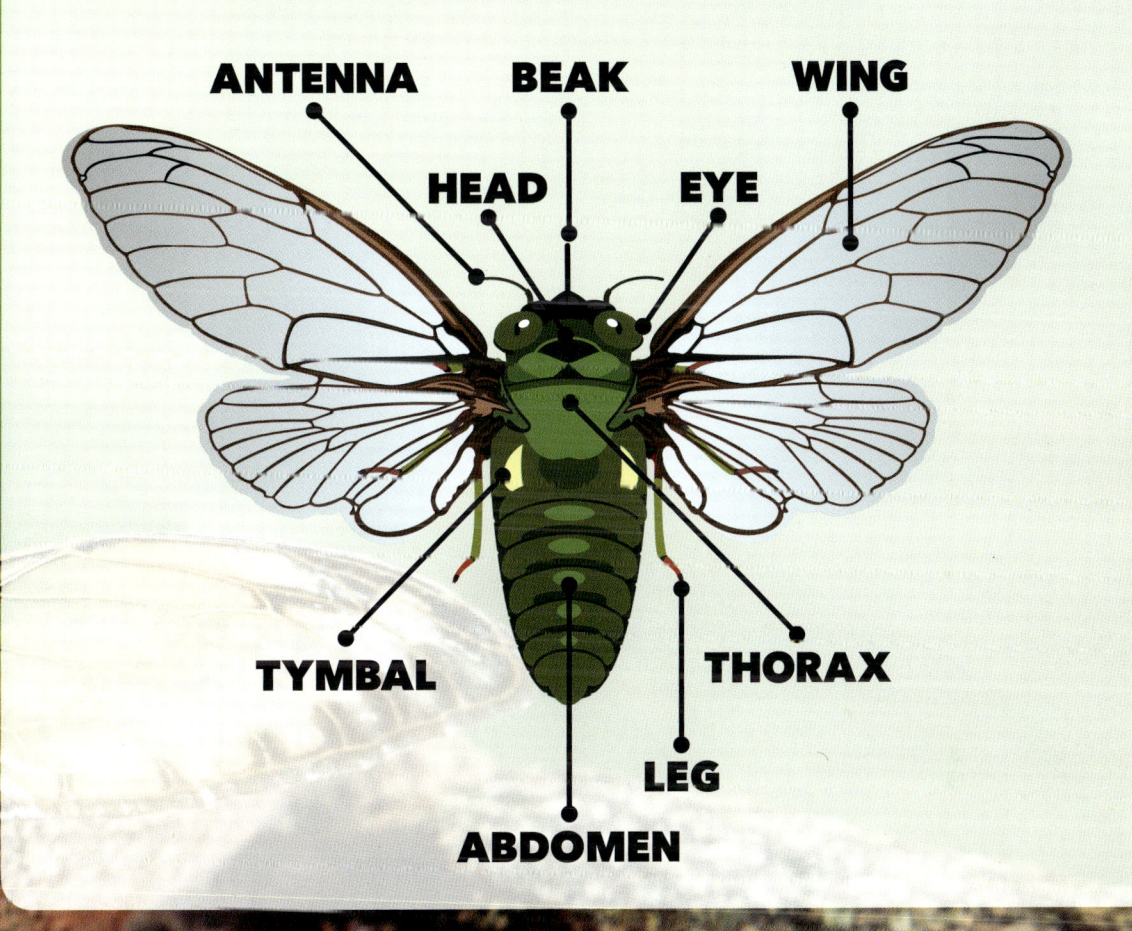

ANTENNA
BEAK
WING
HEAD
EYE
TYMBAL
THORAX
LEG
ABDOMEN

CHAPTER 1   7

CHAPTER 2
LIFE CYCLE

In summer, a female cicada lays up to 400 eggs. She lays them in trees and other plants.

egg

Nymphs hatch after six to ten weeks. They dig underground. Then they stick to plant and tree roots. They drink from the roots.

nymph

CHAPTER 2

9

shed skin

Nymphs **molt** and grow underground. Then they crawl out of the soil. They climb trees. They molt one last time. Now they have wings. They are adults.

TAKE A LOOK!

Cicadas grow in four stages. Take a look!

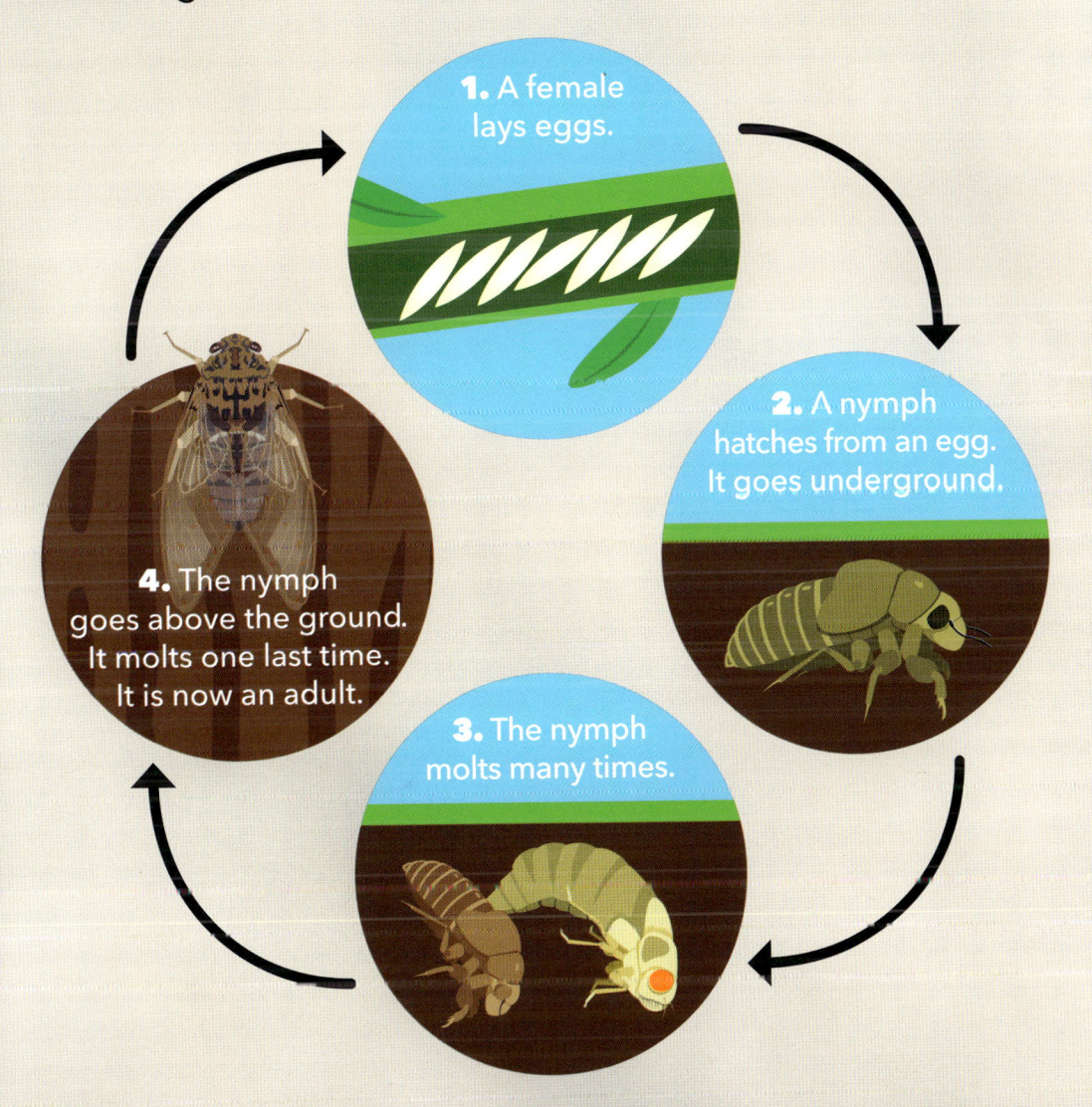

1. A female lays eggs.

2. A nymph hatches from an egg. It goes underground.

3. The nymph molts many times.

4. The nymph goes above the ground. It molts one last time. It is now an adult.

CHAPTER 2

Most cicada species are **annual**. This means the nymphs come out of the ground every year. Others are **periodical**. These nymphs live underground for 13 or 17 years! The adults have red eyes and legs.

DID YOU KNOW?

Periodical cicadas form large **broods**. More than 1 million cicadas can be in one brood. They come up at once. They can cover the size of a football field!

CHAPTER 2

14 CHAPTER 2

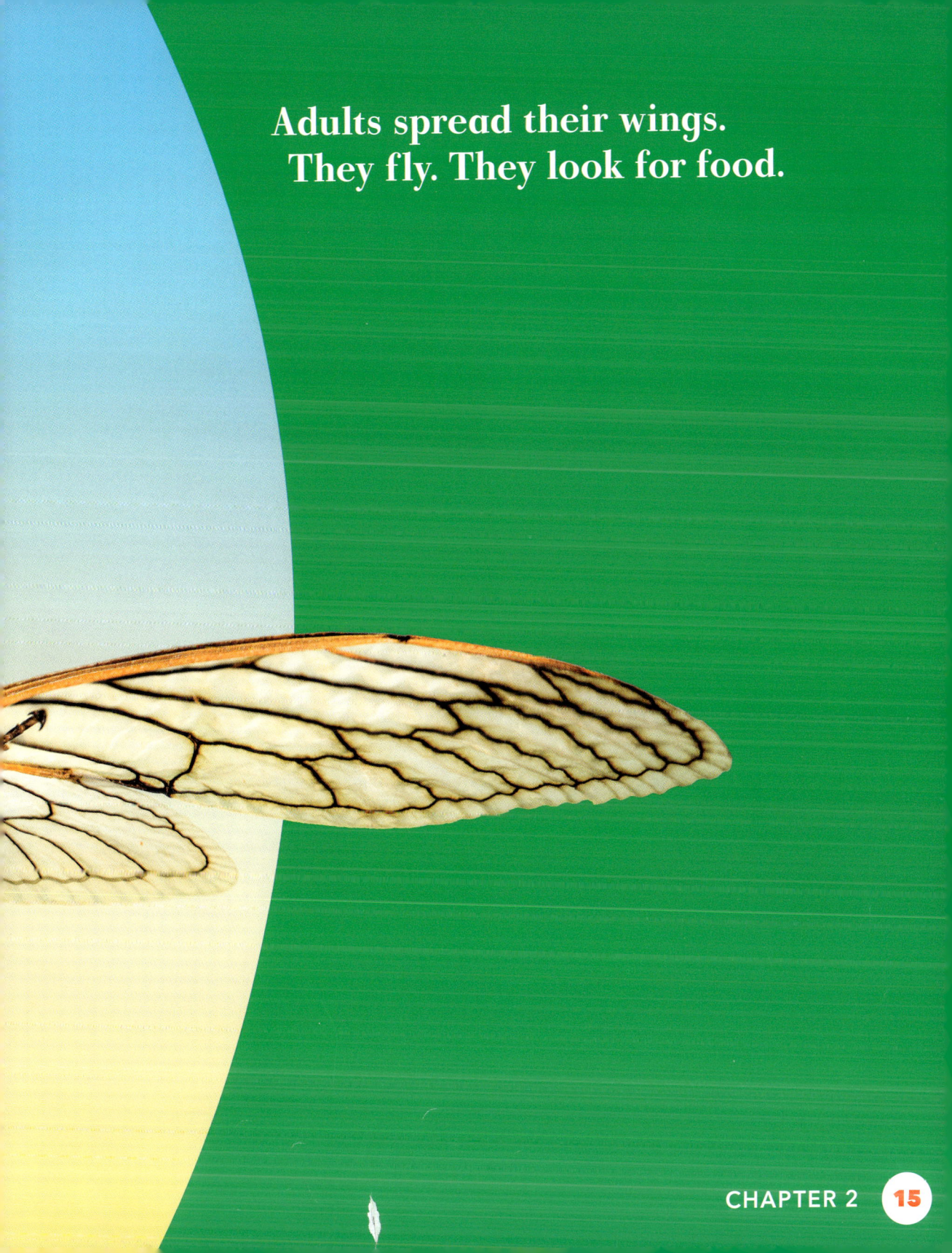

Adults spread their wings. They fly. They look for food.

CHAPTER 2

CHAPTER 3
LIFE ABOVE THE GROUND

Cicadas do not hunk. They use a beak to drink from trees and other plants.

beak

Cicadas fly slowly. They are easy to catch. They do not fight **predators**. Birds, wasps, snakes, and rats eat them.

wasp

CHAPTER 3   17

Adult cicadas only live for a few weeks. Males call to each other. They gather in big groups. Then they call females. Females click their wings. They join the males. The adults **mate**. Females lay eggs.

DID YOU KNOW?

Cicadas have a warning call. They make this sound if danger is close by.

CHAPTER 3

CHAPTER 3

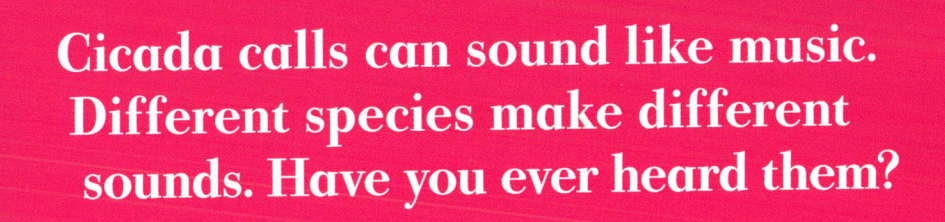

Cicada calls can sound like music. Different species make different sounds. Have you ever heard them?

DID YOU KNOW?

Cicadas are very loud. One cicada can be as loud as a lawn mower!

CHAPTER 3

ACTIVITIES & TOOLS

TRY THIS!

CLOTHESPIN CICADA

Make a cicada in this fun activity!

What You Need:
- cardboard
- pencil
- scissors
- black, green, and red paint
- paintbrush
- clothespin
- black plastic spoon
- black pipe cleaner
- glue

1. Draw four wings on the cardboard. Cut them out.
2. Paint the wings green.
3. Paint the clothespin black.
4. Cut the handle off the spoon. Paint two red eyes on the round part. This is the head.
5. Cut the pipe cleaner in three pieces. Use two to make an X. Place the third one on top to make a star.
6. Open the clothespin. Glue the pipe cleaners inside the groove.
7. Bend the pipe cleaners to make legs.
8. Glue the head to the clothespin.
9. Glue the wings to the clothespin behind the head. Now you have a cicada!

GLOSSARY

annual: Happening every year.

broods: Groups of animals that are born at the same time.

insect: A small animal with three pairs of legs, one or two pairs of wings, and three main body parts.

mate: To come together to produce babies.

molt: To shed an old, outer skin so that a new one can grow.

nymphs: Young cicadas in the larvae stage.

periodical: Happening from time to time.

predators: Animals that hunt other animals for food.

species: One of the groups into which similar animals and plants are divided.

ACTIVITIES & TOOLS

INDEX

abdomen 6, 7
annual 12
beak 7, 16
broods 12
call 18, 21
eggs 8, 11, 18
fly 15, 17
mate 18
molt 10, 11
nymphs 9, 10, 11, 12

periodical 12
plants 5, 8, 9, 16
predators 17
roots 9
species 5, 12, 21
summer 5, 8
trees 8, 9, 10, 16
tymbals 6, 7
underground 5, 9, 10, 11, 12
wings 4, 6, 7, 10, 15, 18

TO LEARN MORE

Finding more information is as easy as 1, 2, 3.

❶ Go to www.factsurfer.com
❷ Enter "cicadas" into the search box.
❸ Choose your book to see a list of websites.

ACTIVITIES & TOOLS